# Santorini

## *The Ultimate Santorini Travel Guide By A Traveler For A Traveler*

## *The Best Travel Tips; Where To Go, What To See And Much More*

# Table of Contents

# Why Lost Travelers Guides?

First, we want to wish you an amazing time in Santorini when you plan to visit. Also we would like to thank you and congratulate you for downloading our travel guide, *"Santorini; The Ultimate Santorini Travel Guide By A Traveler For A Traveler"*.

Tired of long, boring, and biased guides out in the market that not only waste our time but also waste money? So were we! We continuously had to ask someone for the simplest things that could have easily been found if we could speak the language of the location, or information that should have been in the guide we were using at that time! As we continuously face this problem we decided we should create a guide that that would cover everything a traveler needs to know from the point of Arrival to Departure, and the Lost Travelers Guides were born.

When having our guides created we take a lot into consideration such as time, therefore our guides are short and to the point. But mainly we ask ourselves and other travelers what we enjoy during a travel and what we wish we had known prior to visiting the location and that is where the Lost Travelers guides excels. As the Lost Travelers Guide team, we only have one goal and that is to make sure that our guides are the best out, and provides the most value available.

Each one of our guides are created by a team of professional researchers and travelers whom account every detail about the location from a brief history to amazing travel tips including where to go, what to see and much more. Once our guides have been created we then go over and double check to make sure we are providing our travelers with a fun, engaging, informative and the most powerful travel guide on the market.

"The World Is A Book And Those Who Do Not Travel Only Read One Page"

- St. Augustine

Thanks again for choosing us, we hope you enjoy!

# Chapter 1: Brief History

Santorini (pronounced [sando'rini]) is a popular vacation island located in the southern Aegean Sea. It is some 200 km southeast of Greece's mainland and is also the largest of the small archipelago, which shares its name. It is a remnant of what used to be an ancient volcanic caldera.

This archipelago makes up the southernmost point in the region's Cyclades group of islands. The archipelago itself is quite great in size, with an approximate area of 28 sq. mi. as well as a population of 15,550, compiled during a 2011 census. That said, there are islands in this group of islands which are completely uninhabited, including: Kameni, Nea, Palaia, Christiana and Aspronisi. The inhabited municipalities under Santorini include Santorini and Therasia.

Most tourists going to the area are not entirely aware that the island of Santorini is a mere remnant of a powerful volcanic eruption which completely obliterated the various ancient settlements on a previously single island. This explosion also created the geological caldera that we are now familiar with. This huge central lagoon measures some 12 x 7 km and is enclosed by 300 m steep cliffs on three of its sides. Seen in person, it certainly makes for a grandiose sight.

The main islands slope towards the Aegean Sea whilst a much smaller island called Therasia actually separates the lagoon from connecting directly with the sea. It made the lagoon and the sea to meet in two other points, the southwest and northwest points.

The depth of the Santorini caldera prevents any sea vessel except for some of the bigger ships to drop anchor close to the protected bay. That being said, there is also a fisherman's harbor located at Vlychada, right on the island's southwestern coast. Its main port is called Athinias and its capital, Fira, is perched atop a cliff that looks down the lagoon.

Within the South Aegean Volcanic Arc, the archipelago is the main source of volcanic activity, though most of what remains is the caldera we see today. This site is also where one of the most violent volcanic eruptions in history happened. Often referred to as the Minoan eruption, it happened some 3,600 years ago, during the very peak of the Minoan civilization. This left a caldera surrounded by volcanic ash hundreds of meters deep, burying everything beneath it.

This event is thought to have also led to the collapse of the civilization which was wiped out by a tsunami that occurred during its aftermath. Many theorists also believe that this cataclysmic event served as an inspiration for the legendary city of Atlantis.

This isn't the only historical record of the event, however. Even in far flung regions of the earth, the power of the eruption was felt. For example, scientists have begun to correlate a volcanic winter that occurred in China with the Minoan eruption.

Much like the demise of the Minoan civilization, this volcanic winter was also related to the fall of the Xia dynasty. An event which was said to have been accompanied by "a dim sun, yellow fog, frost in July, then three suns, famine and the withering of five cereals."

Moving to more modern times, Santorini was annexed to Greece back in 1912. Major settlements in the area include Oia, Kamari, Fira, Emporio, Therasia, Imerovigli and Pyrgos. There are also many archaeological sites in the area. Akrotiri being the major one that contains ruins dating back to the Minoan era. The island itself is devoid of rivers and water sources can be scarce.

In fact, until the early nineties, the locals who live in it used to collect rain water that fell on their roofs as a means of filling up their tanks. There are small springs, but the residents still needed to import water from other areas of Greece. Today, there is a desalination plant that provides running, but nonpotable, water to many of the homes located in the island.

Santorini's main source of industry is tourism as its pumice quarries have been closed since 1986 as a means of preserving the gorgeous caldera of the island. Aside from tourism, it is also home to a relatively small yet continuously growing wine industry based upon the indigenous grape: Assyrtiko.

The vines of this grape variety are very old and are resistant to phylloxera. If you're a wine lover, a connoisseur, or someone who is looking for something delectable to quench your thirst whilst you take in the breathtaking views of the island then look no further than their locally produced wine.

# Chapter 2: Geography and Climate

## Geological setting

As we have touched upon in the previous chapter, Santorini is an archipelago made up of different volcanic islands. It is this unique location and view that draws many people to it year after year. Its beautiful coastline that stretches to an impressive 69 km surrounds the island and receives plenty of visitors during the summer.

Fira, its capital, has a population of about 13,500 people which makes sure that tourists can enjoy quaint sight-seeing without having to compete with plenty of other people vying to do the same. Needless to say, there is plenty of room for everyone!

Though the event that created the caldera was truly devastating to neighboring areas, one cannot deny the magnificence of what it left behind. This circular caldera is unique in that it is the only sunken one of its kind in the world. In fact, it mostly resembles a lagoon given the fact that it is entirely filled with water.

Surrounding it are gigantic cliffs, upon which many beautiful villages have been built. This is the view that most people are familiar with. White Grecian homes dotting steep cliff sides, creating a truly breathtaking sight.

So, is Santorini in danger of another volcanic eruption any time soon? Well, whilst there is some activity there are no real threats at the moment. In fact, the volcano of Santorini had always provided geologists and scientists with proof of seismic activity through the years and as such, if there ever was a significant possibility of an eruption, there will be plenty of forewarning before it happens.

For now, visitors get to enjoy the culture and architecture of the island, both of which have been influenced by the volcanic activity that happens in the area. Treks are just one of the best activities one can do in order to truly appreciate the unique landscape of the island. From Fira to Oia, there is plenty to see and explore.

Aside from the gorgeous islands created by the volcanic eruptions, the same events have been producing a number of different products which are unique to the region. For example, one would be able to find eruptive products such as rhyolite and basalt which are both associated with volcanic eruptions. These are just some of the rarer souvenirs that you might find whilst going around the different islands.

The islands of and around Santorini are what remains after the repeated sequences of shield volcano construction which subsequently followed the collapse of is caldera. The innermost coast of the caldera itself is actually a precipice, a sheer 985 feet drop featuring varying layers of solidified lava piled on top of each other.

The ground in this area moves down to a slow, outwards and then downwards heading to its outer perimeter where the beaches are both shallow and smooth. The color of the sand in this area highly depends on which geological layer is most exposed. There are those with pebbles or sand containing solidified lava hence the different colors of the sands. Red, black and white sand beaches are all common sights here.

**Climate**

In terms of climate, Santorini is one of the only two locations in Europe that features a hot desert climate. The island typically experiences two different seasons. From April to October, the season is warm and dry. From November to March, however, the season is cold and rainy. Remember these so you will be able to plan your visit to the island around the best season suited to your preferences.

Because there are no land formations such as mountains around Santorini, the island is also often battered by strong winds for most of the year. These are commonly referred to by the locals as "maistros" or northwestern winds. There are also those referred to as "ostria" or south wind. The latter are typically stronger than those coming from the north.

Another important climate feature of Santorini as well as the entirety of the Aegean Sea would be the "Meltemia". These are the annual northwestern or local north winds which arrive around May to September. Many locals consider it as a blessing during the hotter summer days.

It also brings with it a sound that many new tourists to the island often find surprising. You might experience it whilst visiting the caldera or enjoying a view of it— pay attention to the whistling sound which can be heard whenever the Meltemia "visits" the island. There's no need to worry, of course! This is just a normal sound produced by strong winds passing through Santorini.

Lastly, the atmosphere can be extremely humid regardless of the hour. This is because anywhere you stand on the island, the distance between land and sea is no greater than 3km.

**The Best Time to Visit:**

When it comes to sun tanning and swimming, the best time to visit the island would be during its warmest weather. This is between June and September. It can be very sunny, but the temperature is perfect for swimming. You would want to be able to enjoy the warm waters of Santorini, as it certainly is one of the best.

For sightseeing. If you're visiting the island for its famous sights, wineries and food then you don't necessarily need warm weather to enjoy all of that. The months of April, May, October and early November would be the best time for doing all of these. The weather remains warm by Northern European standards and whilst there might be some rain during your visit, it still is tolerable. In fact, it might even be a welcome treat.

Low season. If you're looking to save a bit of money during your visit then make sure that you opt for the low season.

From December to March as well as from April to November, hotel prices tend to be much cheaper. However, don't expect everything else to be priced as low. Food, transportation and drink prices do not change according to season.

The only downside here is that the weather may not be as great as you would want it to be. This is especially true if you're looking forward to lounging by the beach. However, during the first three weeks of October, the weather tends to get warmer so you might find yourself pleasantly surprised during your visit.

High Season. Hot and sunny weather on the island will surely bring with it plenty of people. Prices will be at their peak too. However, the sea water is at its warmest and the island has a lot more activities to offer compared to the low season.

# Chapter 3: Cultural Activities

When it comes to activities, there are plenty of different things that you can do in the gorgeous island of Santorini. Most people visit to enjoy its pristine beaches and to bask in the warm Aegean sun. However, what else can you do if that gets a little too repetitive?

Well, how about learning more about the island's culture and history? From centuries-old churches to gaining more knowledge about the island's ancient inhabitants, here are some of the ways through which you can connect more with Santorini's colorful culture and people.

## Akrotiri Archaeological Site

This archaeological site is among the most important ones in the entirety of the Eastern Mediterranean and fortunately for budding history buffs, it is also open to the public. It would take around two hours to tour the whole site and you'd be excited to see that almost every part of the buildings was able to withstand time, apart from the roofs.

The site provides people with the rare opportunity to walk along the ancient streets and squares of the city as well as visit various dwellings and religious areas. If you ever wanted to see and feel what it was like back then, this is your chance. There are also a number of installations showcasing what life must have been like for people during this time.

Aside from these, you will also find displays showing some of the preserved details that illustrate how the volcanic eruption significantly damaged and eliminated all life from the ancient city of Akrotiri. It is both a tragic yet powerful reminder of how unpredictable nature really is.

The entire site is wheelchair accessible and there is a medical office readily available for those who might need it. Akrotiri can be visited by bus or private car.

## Archaeological Museum of Thera

Another way through which you can connect with the islands rich history is by dropping at this museum. History buffs will definitely get a kick out of all the collections on display. The Archaeological Museum of Thera can be found near the Frankish quarter of Fira. The contemporary building which houses all of the museum's collection is a fairly new one, erected back in the 1960's to replace the 1902 building which was significantly damaged during the 1956 earthquakes that shook the entire island.

There are permanent exhibitions to be explored such as different finds from the ancient city as well cemeteries of Thera. It spans a timeline from the early history of the place to the late Roman times.

Other collections it houses include artifacts including its Proto-cycladic marble figurines which can be dated back to the $3^{rd}$ millennium BC as well as others coming from the Classical period. There are also prehistoric vases taken from Akrotiri which have been dated back to the $17^{th}$ and $20^{th}$ centuries BC.

Getting to the museum is relatively easy as there are plenty of transport services available in and around the city. It is located at Fira, Santorini. Museum hours are at 08:30 – 15:00. Do note that it is closed during Mondays so do time your visit accordingly.

## Bellonio Cultural Centre and Library

Some aspects of the island's culture are best learned through books and there's no better place to do that than the Bellonio Cultural Foundation. This was the brainchild of brothers Lucas and Evangelos Bellonias and was founded back in 1994, after the establishment of its namesake non-profit institution.

The center can be found near Fira's central square and its main goal is to help with promoting the arts as well as literature throughout the island. The library currently houses a grand collection of about 35,000 books, all of which are regularly updated. It is also home to a conference room and a parlour.

The collection and the library are considered by many to be an integral part of Santorini's cultural heritage despite its humble beginnings. It began with no more than 3,000 books coming from the personal collection of its founders. It is their love for the island and the want to improve the level of education provided for its people that urged the brothers to begin this endeavor. The result, of course, is the library which locals and tourists alike may enjoy.

The library is open Monday/Wednesday/Friday 09:00-15:00, Tuesday/Thursday 09:00-14:00 & 17:00-20:00.

## Santorini Wine Museum

What's the best way to wind down after a morning of visiting museums? Well, with a nice glass of wine, of course. Connoisseurs and even the average wine lover would be very glad to know that the island itself has its very own wine museum. Located in the road to Kamari and is the only one of its kind in Greece. The tour itself is impressive, going through the history of wine on the island as well as all the effort that goes into making a single bottle.

But it isn't just the information that's breathtaking for the museum itself is a sight to behold. Located six meters underground and with a length of 300 meters all comprised of different rooms and exhibits. It certainly is a labyrinthine structure that would take you through wine-related history, going back to 1660 and leading into the 1970s.

The goal of the museum is to educate locals and tourists about the history of wine in Santorini as well as its significance when it comes to the island's culture. The tour concludes with a sampling of select wines, making sure that everyone who visits not only gets to see how production happens, but also be able to taste the final results of all the effort put into it. It definitely is a must-visit site!

Opening hours: 12:00-20:00 (April to October) | 09:00-14:30 (November to March)

# Chapter 4: Where to go and What to see

After educating yourself on Santorini's rich history, how about acquainting yourself with its present and trying out all the different activities that the island has to offer? From quiet sightseeing to something more adventurous, there's certainly something for everyone. Here's a quick list to help you get started!

## Catamaran Sunset Cruise

Do know that every tour would be different and would also offer different options for you to try. Some of the options are hiking, swimming, visiting Thirassia to explore its villages, a stop at the White and Red beaches for snorkeling or simply enjoying a meal on the boat. It depends on the kind of trip you're looking for.

There are packages available where you can mix and match some of the options, but make sure you discuss the prices very clearly as this can vary from one activity to the next. If your hotel offers cruises or is affiliated with a local company for it, have them plan out everything for you. This would be the easiest way to go by it.

Meals are also often provided on board whether you chose one that included it or not. These are typically simple yet local fare so you'll get a taste of Santorini cuisine regardless.

## Hike from Fia to Oia

Even if you're not much of a nature buff, this is something that you must do if you're visiting Santorini. Not only is it free of charge, it would offer you some great views and a truly once in a lifetime experience. Do prepare yourself for it can be physically tasking.

The hike itself usually takes 2 to 5 hours depending on your pace. It gets longer if you stops for pictures along the way and this is something that you will inevitably do as the sights are something you simply cannot pass up. The hike starts in Fira and moves northward through Firostefani then Imerovigli. From there going to Oia, the path changes from quaint village pathways to something more rural.

Do wear comfortable shoes and bring water for the journey. Another thing to note is the fact that the route isn't marked, but is fairly easy to follow. Nevertheless, do stay aware of your current location and direction.

## Exploring the paths, stairwells and alleyways of Oia

Santorini is well known for the winding alleyways that comprise its whole and an afternoon of exploring these paths will certainly not disappoint you! Get off the beaten path, grab a map and start visiting places that aren't in any guide. You might surprise yourself with all the hidden gems you'll discover and if not, you can rest assured that there will be splendid views at every turn. It definitely is a must do when you're visiting the island!

## Enjoy the Hot Springs and Walk the Volcano

It's the hot springs that tend to draw people from all corners of the globe to visit the island so this is a one stop that you can't miss. Take a boat to the caldera and jump off of it to swim the rest of the way leading to warmer waters by the volcanic hot springs. Whilst it can get hot there, you will never feel the need to get out. It is also known to be very therapeutic!

Once you're done enjoying the healing waters, why not make the 20 minute walk up an active volcano? Nea Kameni is the island located right in the middle of the caldera. The volcano found on it has a crater that reaches 130 meters and would provide you with an experience that you won't forget.

## Sunset Boat Tour

Aside from the volcano tour, you can also go visit the island of Thirassia as well as the Red and Black beaches. There are plenty of boats leaving the Athinios port everyday or you can find some by the Old Port in Fira. Most hotels can help you arrange this trip to avoid hassles along the way so do discuss it with your concierge.

The best bit about hotel arranged trips is that tour companies will often send a car to pick you up and take you back to your hotel once the trip is done. If you're looking for convenience then this is certainly the way to go.

## Getting Around the Island:

To enjoy all that the island has got to offer, you have to first know how to make your way around it. There are a number of different transportations available.

You can always get around in a rented car or scooter, but if you'd rather give the public transportation a try then you have two options: The bus and the taxis. Here's what you need to keep in mind for both.

- There are bus stops for all the villages in the island and during the summer season, a bus passes through at least every 30 minutes or so. The last trip of the day comes around at midnight. During winter, however, the wait goes up to one hour for every bus and the last bus arrives at 9pm. Fira's central bus station is located near the taxi station.

- The public transportation buses on the island are green. If you see ones of other colors, these are the tourist buses passing through.

- You can find the bus timetables at http://www.ktel-santorini.gr/

- The island's local buses are not equipped with automated machines so you need to have money on you for the fare. The maximum fare for a ride would be 2 euro, depending on where you're headed. Always bring exact change to avoid hassles!

- Whilst there are taxis, they can be quite difficult to find during the summer and are most often more active during the winter season. You can book your ride before you arrive to your destination to make sure that there is one waiting for you. If you're already on the island, you can try booking a taxi at the central office in Fira, but always have a backup plan as this might not always work out in your favor.

# Chapter 5: Best Places to Stay

It all depends on what you're looking for. Is it great views of the island? Some privacy where you can enjoy your mornings without noise? What about somewhere near the best nightspots around? The island of Santorini offers plenty of options when it comes to accommodations so whether you're traveling on a budget or don't mind splurging for something unique and luxurious, you're bound to find the right place to stay.

### *A sunset view hotel or a caldera view hotel?*

Ask anyone who has been to the island before and they'll tell you that a caldera view is the best. It's something you can enjoy all day whilst the sunset only comes once and only lasts for a few minutes. In fact, it is better to enjoy the sunset on the steps of Oia, a wine in hand and in the company of other appreciative tourists.

You will still get to enjoy the sunset even if you choose a room with a caldera view. Imerovigli is the highest point in any village hence it will be able to provide you with the most spectacular views of the caldera.

One of the best hotels when it comes to a caldera view would be the Santorini Grace as it can provide you with breathtaking views from three different directions. That's three different photo opportunities for you to choose from!

Other nearby hotels that are worth checking out include: Kasimatis Studios, Avaton Resort and Spa, and Galaxy Suites. These have the highest perch on the island, ensuring an overall view of the caldera as well as superb sunset views. Why choose when you can have both, right?

Looking for a little solitude? The Aenaon Villas would be the best place for you to stay in. It certainly is a little bit more isolated when compared to the others, but it provides similarly extraordinary views that capture both Oia and Imerovigli within its frame.

## Budget Options:

Alright, so not everyone can afford the hefty price tag that often comes with that perfect view you're looking for. You get what you pay for. This is the general rule when it comes to any hotel in any given country. If you're willing to do a little compromise, however. May it be on the amenities or the view, you'll be able to find really cozy places to stay in for very good value. Here are a few:

Located in Fira are the Kamares Apartments and Keti Hotel, both of which are known to have great views. You can also try Villa Maria Damigou and Villa Ilias in Firostefani. Not all of the rooms have a view, but the rates are certainly easy on the budget. If you're looking for quaint charm, Zoe House and Delfini Villas would provide you with great units as well as some enchanting views in Oia.

If location isn't a big factor for you, then check out the collection of different hotels just a 20 minute walk away from Fira. All of which have a nice perch on the caldera's cliff, guaranteeing great view. Lilium Santorini Villa, Butterfly Villas and Volcano View are just three of your options.

### *When should I book my hotel?*

As important as your hotel options would be to know when to book for your room. Keep in mind that most luxury hotels can be fully booked 6 to 12 months in advance so getting a room a year before your trip is certainly not looking too far ahead. It's only being sensible.

The same goes for weddings which can be fully booked as early as 2 to 3 years in advance. So if you want the best place to stay in or to say your "I do's" as the sun sets on the island then make sure you plan everything early and get your slot as soon as possible.

# Chapter 6: Best Places for Food and Drink

Among Santorini's pride, other than their great natural wonders, would be the food and drink that the island has got to offer. There are many delectable dishes available that will surely have you missing the island itself long after you have gone home.

Now, there are plenty of places to choose from when it comes to food and locals might tell you that each one has a unique charm worth trying. However, since you cannot spend your entire vacation trying out all the restaurants found on the island, here's a quick list for your convenience.

## DIMITRIS

Ammoudi, Santorini

Website: www.dimitris-ammoudi-restaurant.com

Telephone Number: 00 30 22860 71606

One look at the waterfront and you'll be able to spot a number of fish tavernas all competing for your attention. Dimitris wins because they have the friendliest service and the freshest fish in Ammoudi.

## NECTAR & AMBROSIA

Oia, Santorini

Website: www.restaurant-ambrosia.com

Telephone Number: 00 30 22860 71504

As appetizing as its name, this place serves modern Mediterranean food coupled with excellent service. You'll certainly feel right at home if you dine here. Their menu is simple, but the food certainly is some of the best on the island. You might find yourself going back for seconds.

## AKTAION

Firostefani, Santorini

Website: www.aktaionsantorini.com

Telephone Number: 00 30 22860 22336

For 80 years, this tavern has been the go to spot for some average priced dishes and the authentic Santorini atmosphere that everyone wants. Some of its popular dishes include the mackerel fritters, fava with capers and their famous white-aubergine pie.

## ARCHIPELAGOS RESTAURANT

Fira, Santorini

Website: www.archipelagos-santorini.com

Telephone Number: 00 30 22860 24509

This resto is located right beside some of Fira's best, along a Cliffside which also overlooks the caldera. That means you get a gorgeous view of the sunset while you enjoy the dinner being served—which is also one of the best that the town has got to offer. Mediterranean-Greek fare that's sure to tickle your tastebuds!

## 1800

Oia, Santorini

Website: www.oia-1800.com

Telephone Number: 00 30 22860 71485

Another island gem, this restaurant boasts of a 200 year old location and has remained as the top spot in Oia when it comes to dinner—it's been two decades since and the 1800 is still going strong.

## NIKOLAS TAVERNA

Erythrou Stavrou, Fira, Santorini

For something no-frills with a laidback vibe, this tavern is the best place to visit. The meals are very expensive, but are also some of the best in Fira. It is definitely great if you're looking for a more local experience as well.

## FRANCO'S CAFE

Pyrgos, Santorini

Website: www.francos.gr

Telephone Number: 00 30 22860 24428

Looking for some of the finest cappuccinos that the island has to offer? Perhaps some Bellinis? Look no further than this refined café right by the fortress of Pyrgos. It's a great after-adventure stop, just right when you want to wind down.

## Where to DRINK:

## HASAPIKO

Oia, Santorini

Telephone Number: 00 30 22860 71244

Formerly a butcher shop, this very lively and energetic spot is an institution in Oia. It is also better known by the locals as Mary-Kay, the woman who also happens to be the owner of this entertainment center.

## DOMAINE SIGALAS

Oia, Santorini

Website: www.sigalas-wine.com

Telephone Number: 00 30 22860 71644

You will find the finest vintage wine with a side of local snacks to nibble on. It's quaint and relaxed vibe will certainly soothe your tired muscles from all the day's activities. This is one of the best places for couples who are looking for a more secluded and quiet evening.

# Chapter 7: Shopping and Nightlife

Fira is where you'll find the central market of the island and its alleyways is crowded by numerous shops that are sure to satisfy even the most discerning of tastes. This is also where you'll locate what people refer to as the "gold" street, also known as Ypapantis—known to be one of the biggest gold markets in the whole of Greece.

Here you'll be able to find the trendiest jewelry designs and collections from both local and foreign designers. If you're looking for a souvenir that you can wear and keep as an heirloom, then this is certainly the place to get it. Most of the jewelries here are handmade so the price may vary depending on where you're buying.

The market located in Oia is just as important. If you're looking for postcard worthy little shops then here is where you'll find those. You'll be able to find clothing from various local as well as foreign designers in many of these little shops, but it's the artwork and souvenir trinkets that truly stand out. There's plenty to discover here and you'll find that the items for sale not only reflect Santorini's culture, but also that of its neighboring places.

For a cheap yet great memento from the island, bringing back a bottle of their local wine is the best way to go. White wine, also known as Vinsanto is very popular for this purpose. Get one for yourself and a couple more for your friends. It really is one of the best dessert wines around. Do make sure to buy yours from a direct producer and don't be afraid to ask for a sample taste.

## Nightlife:

A day of shopping calls for some partying after sundown and Santorini will certainly not disappoint. There are plenty of places to go which offers visitors with unique experiences each time. Here are some of the island's most popular nightlife spots.

## Kira Thira

The oldest and one of the firsts in town, but is also the most diverse when it comes to entertainment. There's blues music, some jazz, Latin and even ethnic music is regularly played. The house's most popular drink that you must certainly try would be the Sangria. It is the perfect drink after a long day under the sun.

Location: Erythroú Stavroú

Hours: 8pm onwards, open on most days of the year

Telephone Number: 00 30 22860 22770

## Enigma

Another oldie, but goodie. Enigma plays a soundtrack of both house and mainstream fare. It is the place to go for many local youth given its outdoor bar and relaxed vibe. It also has a significantly gay clientele.

Location: Erythroú Stavroú

Hours: 11pm onwards, from June to early part of September

Website: facebook.com/EnigmaClubSantorini

Telephone Number: 00 30 22860 22466

## Koo Club

This one is made for larger parties. Their indoor space can accommodate 300 and they have outdoor verandas where you'll be able to find 3 different bars serving the crowd. It's mostly a dance club, but they also host a number of special events and would often invite DJ's for certain evenings.

Location: Erythroú Stavroú

Hours: 11pm onwards, from May to early part of September

Website: kooclub.gr

Telephone Number: 00 30 22860 22025

**Potamos**

If you're not into dancing or loud music then head on over to this quiet garden café. It will treat you to some relaxing acoustic music and some really great food—though the menu is a little over on the expensive side. It is still worth it.

Hours: 7pm onwards, from mid-April to late part of October

Website: facebook.com/Potamos.ia

Telephone Number: 00 30 22860 72045

# Chapter 8: Unique Experiences

### Go cliff jumping at Amoudi Bay

Looking for a little thrill during your stay? Well, what do you think about jumping into the crystal clear waters of the island, all whilst you're surrounded by breathtaking cliff faces? If that appeals to you, head on out to Amoudi Bay and its swimming spots where you can unleash your inner dare devil by cliff jumping. This is one of those must-do things when you're on the island. Just make sure you're capable of doing it and that you know how to swim—basic things, of course.

TO GET THERE: This is a fairly hidden gem and would certainly require a bit of legwork as you need to climb quite a bit in order to get to it. However, all that work is worth it—for the experience as well as the view that will greet you is definitely one that's unforgettable. Besides, if you're not up for some cliff jumping then simply getting a tan on by the rocks is just as worthwhile.

### Hire a quad bike and drive around the island

Here's one for the explorers and adventurers. Ready to take on the island? Crush down its winding roads and find hidden gems along the way. This particular activity is also one of the most affordable ones that you can enjoy on the island so do make sure that you take full advantage of it! Bring a group along, it's best enjoyed with a company.

### Stay in a Cave house

You've seen those cave houses in every postcard and photo of the Greek islands. Well, this time, why not try staying in one? There are plenty of hostels that would be able to provide you with this experience as well as some very traditional activities that should bring you closer to the island's heart. Learn new things from the locals and appreciate your stay in a deeper way.

There are a number of places where you might find this so doing a bit of research in advance would certainly help you pick the ones which fit your preferences best. The prices tend to vary according to the season too so make sure you get in touch with the proprietor to avoid surprises in your credit card.

If you're looking for something authentically Greek, it doesn't get any better than spending a few nights in one of its many traditional homes.

## Get the perfect spot to watch the most famous sunset of the world

Alright, so the sunset is a pretty given one, but never write it off as a cliché experience. There are many different ways through which you can enjoy this gift of nature and during your stay on the island, you'll definitely find the best ones. The only thing you need to make sure of is to avoid the crowds as having an isolated spot for yourself is the best way to really enjoy this spectacular view.

Have a picnic with friends and watch as the sun goes down. It will be a pinch-yourself kind of moment and a memory you'll definitely carry for the rest of your life. With just a bottle of wine, some delicious snacks and great company, even the simplest of pleasures can turn into something grand.

# Chapter 9: Survival Guide

## Currency:

The monetary unit that Greece uses is the EURO and there are no other currencies accepted in this territory. It is advisable that you get your money exchanged before you even travel to the country in order to make sure that you have enough for emergencies and other needs as soon as you land.

Typically, bank exchange rates remain the same throughout the country—but only if you do it at an official bank exchange. There are smaller establishments that might offer higher rates, but there is always a risk involved with this. Do keep in mind that money changers in tourist areas will charge very high commissions and it would do you good to avoid these places unless you really need cash.

Remember, you will need some local currency at the airport in order to pay for certain necessities, particularly the luggage carts if you need it.

Now, some people do use traveler's checks and whilst this is accepted in most places, do make note that not all shops take them. This is especially so if you're dealing with smaller shops or places that's off the tourist track. In fact, a few shop keeps may not even know what traveler's checks are so be prepared with extra cash.

The best way to get some money whilst you're in Greece would be through ATM machines. These can be found just about everywhere and on any island so you can ease some of your worries. If you have a debit card that also doubles as a visa, this makes things a lot easier for you.

Most hotels and restaurants will accept cards, but do keep in mind that the town shops might not. You'll be able to tell which ones do by the signs at their doors. The same applies for places where you get basic needs such as gas—there are pumps that have signs on them indicating that credit cards are accepted. However, there are places that only take cash.

**Safety Tips:**

- As with most tourist destinations, it is important to keep your valuables in check. If you have travel wallets, do make use of them and always be aware of your surroundings. There are various traveler bags and wallets that come with safety features which help prevent thieves from getting to your things—but if you're not careful, you can still lose some stuff by your own negligence.

- New to the city? Make sure you always carry a map with you and have someone from your hotel, write down the address in the local language. Whilst it's great to try and walk on the off-beaten path, it's still best to stick to the areas where there are plenty of people and you're still familiar with. Always keep your wits about you and refrain from going into shady looking areas on your own.

- If you do experience a threat or think that you are being followed, walk with confidence and find the nearest establishment that looks safe. If there are tourists in it, it is likely your next best option. Don't bring your map out until you're in the safe zone and find someone who can lead you back to a more populated area if you really did lost your way. A little bit of awareness goes a long way if you're traveling to foreign destinations.

- Here's the golden rule, leave your valuables at home. If you don't have to dress up, don't wear fancy jewelry. This only makes you more attractive as a target for would-be thieves. If your hotel provides you with a safe, make use of it.

## Emergencies:

- Fira Health Centre - (+30) 2286 022237

- Emporio First Aid Station - (+30) 2286 081222

- Kamari First Aid Station - (+30) 2286 031175

- Oia First Aid Station - (+30) 2286 071227

- Pyrgos First Aid Station - (+30) 2286 031207

- Thirassia First Aid Station (- (+30) 2286 029144

- Fira Pharmacy - (+30) 2286 022700

- Fira Police - (+30) 2286 022649

- Oia Police - (+30) 2286 071954

- Fire Brigade - (+30) 2286 033199

## Insider Tips:

This might seem pretty intuitive, but do bring sunglasses on your trip. Those white-washed streets and homes may look picture perfect but they can be quite blinding in person. Another thing, always bring comfortable shoes—heels will not cut in the streets of Santorini unless you'll be chauffeured from your every destination to the next.

Lastly, do appreciate the local vendors and always buy something from them whenever possible. Stop for the old winemakers, you'll know them by their stained fingertips, and get some souvenir Vinsanto from them. Not only will you be getting some of the best, you're also helping these people with their livelihood.

And really, what better way to leave a place that has given you so much to take in than to leave some kindness before you go? After all, it's about the give and take. Traveling anywhere in the world will teach you that.

# Conclusion

Once again thank you for choosing *Lost Travelers*!

I hope this book was able to provide you with the best travel tips when visiting Santorini.

*And we hope you enjoy your travels.*

"Travel Brings Power And Love Back To Your Life"

- Rumi

Finally, if you enjoyed this book, then I'd like to ask you for a favor, would you be kind enough to leave a review for this book on Amazon? It'd be greatly appreciated!

- ➤ Simply search the keywords "Santorini Travel Guide" on Amazon or go to our Author page "Lost Travelers" to review.

Your satisfaction is important to us! If you were not happy with the book please email us with the title, your comment and suggestion so we may consider any improvements and serve you better in the next edition.

- ➤ Email: SevenTreeImprove@gmail.com

Thank you and good luck!

# NOTES

# NOTES

# NOTES

# NOTES

# Preview Of 'New Zealand: The Ultimate New Zealand Travel Guide By A Traveler For A Traveler

Located 2,012 km to the south of Australia is New Zealand. There are two main islands comprising it, the North and South islands, and outlying islands scattered within the vicinity. Its two main islands are separated by a body of water known as the Cook Strait. The North Island is 829 km long. Its southern end is volcanic and because of this, there are plenty of excellent hot springs and geysers in the area. On the South island, lies the Southern Alps by the west end. Here is where one will find the highest point in New Zealand which is Mount Cook. It is 12,316 feet tall!

Some of the outlying islands are inhabited while others are not. The inhabited islands include Chatham, Great Barrier, and Stewart islands. The largest of the uninhabited islands are Campbell, Kermadec, Antipodes, and Auckland islands.

The first inhabitants of New Zealand were the Maoris. Their initial population was only 1,000 people. According to their oral history, it took the initial Maori population seven canoes to reach New Zealand from other parts of Polynesia. It was in the mid-1600s that the island cluster was explored by a man named Abel Tasma, a Dutch navigator. Another foreigner, a British by the name of James Cook, engaged in three voyages to New Zealand the first one taking place in 1769. New Zealand became a formal annex to Britain during the mid 1800s.

During this time, the Treaty of Waitangi was signed between Britain and the Maoris. It stated that there will be ample protection for Maori land should the Maoris accept British rule. Despite the treaty, tension between both factions intensified over time due to the continuous encroachment by British settlers.

Check out the rest of New Zealand: The Ultimate New Zealand Travel Guide on Amazon by simply searching it.

# Check Out Our Other Books

Below you'll find some of our other popular books that are on Amazon and Kindle as well. Simply search the titles below to check them out. Alternatively, you can visit our author page (Lost Travelers) on Amazon to see other work done by us.

- ➢ Vienna: The Ultimate Vienna Travel Guide By A Traveler For A Traveler

- ➢ Barcelona: The Ultimate Barcelona Travel Guide By A Traveler For A Traveler

- ➢ London: The Ultimate London Travel Guide By A Traveler For A Traveler

- ➢ Istanbul: The Ultimate Istanbul Travel Guide By A Traveler For A Traveler

- ➢ Vietnam: The Ultimate Vietnam Travel Guide By A Traveler For A Traveler

- ➢ Peru: The Ultimate Peru Travel Guide By A Traveler For A Traveler

- ➢ Australia: The Ultimate Australia Guide By A Traveler For A Traveler

- ➢ Japan: The Ultimate Japan Travel Guide By A Traveler For A Traveler

- ➢ New Zealand: The Ultimate New Zealand Travel Guide By A Traveler For A Traveler

- ➢ Dublin: The Ultimate Dublin Travel Guide By A Traveler For A Traveler

- ➢ Thailand: The Ultimate Thailand Travel Guide By A Traveler For A Traveler

- ➢ Iceland: The Ultimate Iceland Travel Guide By A Traveler For A Traveler

- ➢ Santorini: The Ultimate Santorini Travel Guide By A Traveler For A Traveler

- ➢ Italy: The Ultimate Italy Travel Guide By A Traveler For A Traveler

You can simply search for these titles on the Amazon website to find them.

Made in United States
North Haven, CT
15 June 2022

20272848R00028